BR BLUE No...

TRAIN FORMAT...

John Dedman

N.B.

ISBN 978-1-909328-15-0

First published in 2014 by Kevin Robertson
under the **NOODLE BOOKS** imprint
PO Box 279
Corhampton
SOUTHAMPTON
SO32 3ZX

www.noodlebooks.co.uk

Printed in England by Berforts Information Press.

Front cover: No 37176 is heading south from Burton-on-Trent towards Wichnor Junction, it is the 6M97 08:22 Tinsley to Wolverhampton Steel Terminal. The formation has a good mix of steel carrying wagons and includes three SPAs, a BDA, a Sliding Hood steel coil wagon and five BBA steel coil wagons with sheeted loads. 19th June 1986.

Preceding page: No On the 27th July 1984 33030 is passing Nursling with a Portsmouth Harbour to Cardiff train composed of five Mk1 coaches. The first coach is a corridor composite followed by four second class coaches, the last of which is a brake second.

Rear cover: No 46016 heads south from Worcester with the 9V66 Bescot to Gloucester New Yard unfitted wagonload freight train on 22nd July 1983. There is an interesting selection of wagons as the train consists of two HTV with coal load, empty tube wagon, empty MCV coal wagon, an OBA open wagon, a class A TEB bogie petroleum tank wagon no. 84035, a Sheerness Steel PXA bogie scrap wagon, a TTA bitumen tank, three BP Class A TTA tanks and a BR brake van. The front view of this train was shown in BR Blue No 2.

Unless otherwise stated, all photographs are by the Author.

Introduction

Welcome to BR Blue No.6. This volume is different to the previous books as it is not restricted to any particular area or type of train, but the photos are still from the same time period as the previous volumes which is mostly the 1980s.

I have received many compliments on my previous volumes, many of which indicated that they were a good guide to train formations for railway modellers. This gave me the inspiration to compose this volume with railway modellers in mind. I have been a serious railway modeller myself since the mid-1970s and have always looked at the real railway for ideas and inspiration which led me into railway photography. I model two era's myself, the late 1950s to early 1960s Southern Region and 1980s British Rail as seen in this book.

I have read letters in model railway magazines and emails from model railway internet forums asking what coaches or wagons can I run with particular loco classes or loco liveries. With this thought in mind I have selected photos which illustrate complete train formations in most cases. Some, which do not show all of the stock, are block trains with the same type of wagon throughout the train or passenger trains with coaches of the same type.

The photos are arranged by types of traffic, starting with passenger trains followed by parcels and then freight trains.

During the 1980s there were still plenty of loco hauled passenger trains running mostly on cross country services. The formations varied with routes, inter-regional trains from the south coast or south west to Scotland and the north could be composed of up to twelve coaches. Some cross country services were regularly composed of four or five Mk1 coaches quite often behind a class 31 or 33 loco although other classes were also used. Traditionally passenger trains were made up with a brake coach at each end of the formation, which would also include first class accommodation somewhere in the train. By the 1980s formations had changed and a single brake coach sufficed for most services and was often in the centre of the formation. This was useful for the guard to be in the centre of the train especially at some of the short platforms on cross country routes. The first class accommodation was usually confined to one coach, often near the centre of the train. Only the long distance services had any type of catering or buffet cars and they would usually be central in the train with the first class accommodation.

Loco hauled passenger trains to and from London, especially the electrically hauled Euston trains, were made up differently. The first class coaches were usually at the London end of the formation with the standard accommodation at the country end and the catering coaches between the two; the brake coach could be at either end. This information is a guide as it is from my own observations and photographs and not strict rules, as formations seemed to vary a great deal.

Parcel trains were still quite common and formations could be any size from one or two vans upwards. Most of the trains were made up of Mk1 BGs and GUVs as most pre-nationalisation vans and four wheel vans were withdrawn from service in the late 1970s.

The freight trains have been put in the following order, Freightliner, Mixed freight, Coal, Steel, Petroleum, Cement, Construction and Departmental. This roughly follows the Railfreight Sectorisation system which was introduced in October 1987.

Freight train formations vary enormously according to requirements and most types of freight train could be anything from one wagon to a block train of around forty wagons such as HAAs in a Merry Go Round coal train.

Some of the photos show formations which were not normally expected, such as short rakes of HAA wagons and HAA wagons mixed with other types such as HEA wagons. Also included are a lot of the shorter formations which are suitable for the space-starved modellers who cannot always run long formations. Most types of freights regularly appeared in short formations usually as trip workings to the larger yards, these include coal, petroleum, cement, china clay, steel and M.O.D.

Ballast and other types of Departmental workings appeared in all sizes with a great variety of wagons as can be seen in the photos towards the rear of this book.

I realize that not all of the coaches and wagons in the photos are available as ready to run or kit built items but so many new models are becoming available these days that you never know what is around the corner. I would certainly still like to see models produced of some of the rolling stock shown in this book.

I have used codes for coaches and vans which were listed in BR Blue No.5 and TOPS codes for freight wagons which were briefly explained in BR Blue No.3.

The photos in this volume are from 1977 to 1990

I have used some photos from enthusiast friends and they are credited on the captions, this has given the book a better geographical balance and variation of train types. For these I am very grateful to Dave Payne for his 1970s Western Region photos, also Peter Mantle, Keith Mantle, John Fox, Pete Nurse and Pete Moody who have all filled some gaps in my own collection.

The photos were all scanned from 35mm colour slides and negatives.

John Dedman, Brockenhurst 2014

I would like to dedicate this book to my wife Janet for her help and support when compiling the volumes in this series. Also to our sons Jez and Chris for having to grow up with railways, real and model, all three of them are seen here watching the VSOE stock on an excursion. The locomotives are class 73s Nos 73142 'Broadlands' and 73129 'City of Winchester' speeding through Grateley on 16th April 1983.

Passenger Trains

The 06:30 Cardiff to Portsmouth Harbour is passing under Horseshoe Bridge in Southampton behind No 33043. The five Mk1 coaches are a second, a corridor composite, two brake seconds and another second. 25th September 1986.

Opposite top - An unidentified 33/0 with miniature snowploughs is passing Southampton Up Yard with a Bristol to Portsmouth service formed of four Mk1 coaches on 30th June 1984. In the background is No 73108 waiting to depart with Rugby Cement wagons forming the 6Y80 09:46 Southampton Up Yard to Halling.

Opposite bottom - No 47639 'Industry Year 1986' is passing Southampton Up Yard with the heavy twelve coach 08:34 Poole to Edinburgh and Glasgow 'Wessex Scot' on 19th September 1986. The train is composed of mostly air conditioned Mk2 coaches with two brake firsts and a MK1 Miniature Buffet and a MK1 BG at the rear. The Up Yard is still busy with a good variety of wagons on show in the background.

This page - No 33062 is passing Millbrook station with a Portsmouth Harbour to Cardiff train consisting of five Mk1 coaches. From the loco the coaches are SK, CK, BSK, DSK and SK. Trees have grown up along the fence line since this photo was taken and today Freemantle church is almost hidden from this viewpoint. Photo by Peter Mantle

Opposite top - On 21st April 1981 the 2B20 07:56 Brockenhurst to Eastleigh stopping passenger train is approaching Beaulieu Road station for its next stop. The loco is No 73101 which was named 'Brighton Evening Argus' at Brighton station on 3rd December 1980 to celebrate the newspaper's centenary. The coach formation follows the traditional Southern Railway three coach set with two Mk1 BSK brake seconds and a CK corridor composite in the centre.

Opposite bottom - No 73115 has just departed Brockenhurst station with the 07:56 to Eastleigh on 24th August 1979. The three Mk1 coaches are followed by a BR GUV and an ex LMS BG.

This page - On Sunday 7th May 1989 Southampton Tunnel was closed for engineering work and diversions were in place, No 33101 is powering class 442 unit No 2416 near Nursling with a diverted Weymouth to Waterloo service. Photo by Keith Mantle.

Top - Class 491 4TC set number 417 is being propelled through Grateley by push pull fitted 33118; the service is the 08:40 Salisbury to Waterloo.

Right - Looking a bit worse for wear, No 86237 is passing Bushey with an up service on 7th April 1983. Later on in the same year this loco was named 'Sir Charles Halle' after the 19th century pianist. It is hauling a typical West Coast main line set of coaches which includes four first class Mk2s behind the Mk1 BG; the first class coaches were usually formed at the London end of Euston expresses.

Top - Heading north through Bushey is No 87026 which was named 'Sir Richard Arkwright' who was an eighteenth century inventor in the cotton industry. The top speed for these class 87 locos was 100mph which was later increased to 110mph when their cross arm pantographs were replaced with high speed versions. The train is made up of a smart set of Mk2 air conditioned coaches in blue/grey livery. 7th April 1983.

Right - Stratford class 47 No 47571 passing Harlow with an up train from Cambridge on 23rd April 1984. Behind the loco are two Mk1 BGs, the air conditioned coach set also includes a Mk1 RMB and an earlier Mk2 first class coach.

Deltic No 55022 'Royal Scots Grey' is heading towards King Cross at Brookmans Park with eight coaches on 9th October 1979. The train consists of air conditioned Mk2 stock apart from the Mk1 BG behind the loco and the fourth coach which is a Mk1 RKB kitchen buffet.

With its grey roof showing it is a Stratford loco No 47553 is heading south towards Barrow Hill on 7th July 1987. The five Mk1 corridor coaches behind the loco are a BCK brake composite, three SK corridor second, and a BSK brake second.

Top - No 47519 heading north from Barrow Hill at Foxlow Junction with a research train made up of a Mk2 First, a Mk2 Research coach and a BG. 4th July 1985

Right - The 1S49 07:25 Nottingham to Glasgow Central and Edinburgh is passing Clay Cross Junction. The loco is No 47550 'University of Dundee' and shows its Scottish ownership with a Scottie dog emblem on the bodyside and miniature snowploughs. Some of the coaches are branded Scotrail. 4th July 1985.

Opposite top - On 7th September 1987 No 31423 is southbound at Willington with five Mk1 coaches, a brake second, three seconds and a corridor composite.

Opposite bottom - An unusual combination for a double header with Nos 37244 and 31425 heading north at Willington with five Mk1 and Mk2 coaches. 7th September 1987.

Top - Consecutively numbered class 31/4s Nos 31428 and 31429 are heading north at Toton with a class 114 DMU on 30th April 1987. In the background is a wagon works which at that time was overhauling HEA coal wagons

Above - On the 19th June 1986 No 47610 is approaching Wichnor Junction with the 08:35 Leeds to Birmingham New Street service, the eight coach train is made up of a Mk1 BG, Mk2 First, and six Mk2 TSO, the first of which includes a microbuffet. The loco carries a Eastfield Depot Scottie dog logo on the bodyside.

Opposite top - Nos 20145 and 20228 are paired up at Wellingborough with the 1T14 St Pancras to Leicester on the InterCity Diesel day, 21st May 1989. Photo by Keith Mantle.

Opposite bottom - No 45025 is heading south near Cheltenham with nine Mk1 coaches, the first coach is a BG followed by two seconds, a Corridor first , a RMB miniature buffet and the rest look to be more seconds. 9th June 1978.

A well weathered No 50019 'Ramillies' is heading south at Bredon , near Cheltenham with an Inter-Regional train composed of mainly Mk2 air conditioned coaches with the addition of a Mk1 BG and Buffet Car making a total load of eleven coaches. 22nd July 1983.

10 August 1979, 10:46am at Frome, Clink road junction. No 31422 leaves the Frome line on the 09:11 Weymouth to Bristol service. Photo by Dave Payne.

No 31307 has just departed from Frome and is rejoining the West of England main line at Clink Road Junction with a Weymouth to Bristol train on 22nd October 1977; an interesting formation with three Mk1 coaches and a GWR Siphon G van. John Dedman Collection.

Top - With a selection of Mk1 and Mk2 coaches forming the 08:15 Plymouth to Leeds service, No 46032 is seen near Bradford on Tone on 30th May 1980. Photo by Dave Payne.

Bottom - No 50007 'Hercules' named after a 'Colossus' class battleship, is heading past Castle Cary with the summer only 11:25 Plymouth to Paddington service on 10 August 1979. The set of Mk2 air conditioned coaches includes a MK1 BG behind the loco and a MK1 Buffet car after the two first class coaches. In February 1984 50007 was repainted into GWR Brunswick green and renamed 'Sir Edward Elgar' to commemorate the 50th anniversary of the composer's death. Photo by Dave Payne.

No 50006 "Neptune" speeds past Tiverton Junction on the 1M22 09:00 Penzance to Manchester Piccadilly service on 26th June 1982. The coaches are mostly air conditioned Mk2s apart from the Mk1 BG behind the loco which is followed by an early Mk2, the fifth coach is the only first class and the sixth coach is a Mk1 miniature buffet RMB. No 50006 was one of the early class 50 withdrawals from service in 1987 and was cut up later that year. Photo by Dave Payne.

Left - At 9:20am on the 13th June 1981 No 46009 is passing Aller Junction, near Newton Abbot on the 09:02 Paignton to Newcastle service consisting of ten Mk1 coaches, the fourth coach is a corridor composite and the fifth a brake second, the remainder being seconds. Just 3 years later 46009 was utilised for a 100mph crash test into a nuclear flask on a section of the Midland Railways main line track at Old Dalby. Photo by Dave Payne.

With eight Mk1 coaches in tow No 50004 'St Vincent' is passing the camping coaches at Dawlish Warren with the 17:25 Exeter to Paignton on 16th May 1986. The fourth coach is a brake second and the fifth is a corridor composite, the rest of the train are second class coaches.

Top - In the evening sun No 50013 'Agincourt' is approaching the stop at Dawlish Warren with the 16:40 Paignton to Exeter-St-Davids local stopping train. It is made up of four Mk1 coaches, a second, a brake second, a corridor composite and another second class.   Two tankers can be seen anchored on the horizon 12th May 1986.

Bottom - No 50005 Collingwood is passing Cockwood Harbour with a rake of Mk1 coaches which will form the 19:40 Exeter to Waterloo, the empty coaches have come from Plymouth as the 5O26 17.22 Laira to Exeter. 15th May 1986

Top - On some Motorail services the passenger's cars were carried on dedicated car workings with the passengers travelling on normal service trains. One of these was the 1B28 07:30 Paddington to St Austell which has just passed Cogload Junction behind 50050 'Fearless' in plain blue livery. This was a weekend service which only ran on Friday and Saturday and on 26th June 1982 it was quite lightly loaded. Photo by Dave Payne.

Bottom - The 1A77 14:50 St Austell to Paddington Motorail behind No 50050 'Fearless' has just overtaken the 17:55 Taunton to Bristol local DMU at Cogload Junction on 26th June 1982. Photo by Dave Payne.

Opposite top - No 08410 is shunting an InterCity liveried High Speed Train power car at Bristol Temple Meads. Photo by Pete Nurse.

Opposite bottom - No 31467 has a High Speed train power car and a Mk2 departmental brake coach in tow at Wichnor Junction on 11th June 1986. The power car is probably being taken to Derby Works for attention.

Parcel and Van Trains

No 31401 is working hard as it approaches Cogload Junction with the 3A27 06:15 Plymouth to Paddington Parcels on 26th June 1982. The set of ten blue GUVs is broken by a single blue/grey BG which would contain the guard's accommodation. Some Eastleigh drivers who came across the class referred to them as not being able to 'pull the skin off a rice-pudding' comparing them unfavourably to their beloved Class 33s. To be fair this was probably based on prejudice as the Class 31 was certainly a long-lived diesel type. Photo by Dave Payne.

The 06:35 Plymouth to Paddington parcels has a selection of vans in the consist with six blue GUVs, two blue/grey BGs and a single newly painted blue Siphon G. The train is hauled by a very clean No 31158 at Castle Cary on the 9th August 1980. Photo by Dave Payne.

No 47151 is powering through Castle Cary station with the 3A27 06:15 Plymouth to Paddington Parcels on 28th July 1984. The vans are mostly blue GUVs with a blue/grey BG in the centre and a blue BG towards the rear. In the background is the unique white painted 1942 signal box, soon to be swept away by M.A.S. Photo by Dave Payne.

Above - Recently named 'City of Oxford' No 47627 is heading east at Magor in South Wales with a parcels service consisting of four GUV vans on 24th July 1985.

Opposite top - No 81017 is rolling into Crewe from the south with a parcels service on 14th April 1989. The two General Utility Vans are in plain blue livery which obviously have not be cleaned for many months. Photo by Pete Moody.

Opposite bottom - No 81018 is passing Bushey with just two Mk1 BGs heading towards Euston on 7th April 1983.

Left - The 5B60 10:39 Southampton to Clapham Yard N.P.C.C.S. is approaching Eastleigh behind No 33045 on Friday 13th June 1986. All the vans are GUVs apart from the first which is a BG and the fifth which is a Post Office Sorting Van. The tracks on the left lead to Eastleigh diesel depot and carriage sidings, on the right are stored some older vans in departmental service. Photo by Peter Mantle.

Bottom - No 47199 is speeding south towards Clay Cross Junction with Parcels vans on 16th July 1986, the stock is a mixture of blue / grey Mk1 BGs and plain blue GUVs. Avenue sidings can be seen on the right.

No 33027 'Earl Mountbatten of Burma' is heading south towards Southampton at St Denys with two Guvs and an all blue BG on 16th June 1988.

The 4B46 Sunday 11:40 Bournemouth to Clapham Parcels and empty coaching stock is passing Sway in the New Forest. The locos are Nos 73138 and 73140 in large logo livery, the train is composed of BGs and GUVs with Mk1 coaches at the rear. Photo by Keith Mantle.

Freight Workings

Above - Unusual power for a Freightliner train is No 73141 in large logo livery with an unidentified down service passing Eastleigh Yard in July 1985. Photo by Peter Mantle.

Opposite top - A pair of Stratford allocated split headcode class 37s Nos 37038 and 37047 are seen passing South Otterington on 5th July 1988. This is quite a short train by Freightliner standards with what appears to be two sets of five flats. After privatisation 37038 became a DRS loco working mainly nuclear waste flask trains.

Opposite bottom - No 47012 is heading south near Cheltenham with a train of six wheeled milk tanks. 9th June 1978

No 31308 is travelling south towards Wichnor Junction with a single brake van on 19th June 1986. Ninety minutes later it returned heading towards Burton upon Trent with four STV tube wagons and the brake van. A week earlier this same working was hauled by a class 45 number 45118.

It is Tramway Crossing, St.Blazey early morning on 6th July 1987. No 47373 has been dragged from St Blazey Yard by No 37235 and is now reversing to head to Par, where it will reverse again and No 37235 will take the train west and return the empties to Parkandillack for reloading. Ponts Mill Clay Terminal can be glimpsed in the background, lit by the early morning sun 6th July1987. Photo by Pete Nurse.

At 10:08 on 11 August 1978, No 46016 is slowly ascending eastwards towards Dainton tunnel on mixed freight vacuum braked train. Behind the loco are ten china clay wagons followed by a single van and some CPV cement Pressflow wagons. Photo by Dave Payne. Later on the same date the same train is seen at 16:00 at Cockwood harbour with No 45019 at the helm. The locos were probably changed at Newton Abbott where the train stopped for a few hours. Photo by Dave Payne.

Speedlink

No 47270 is at Magor with a good selection of wagons heading for Severn Tunnel Junction yard. The wagons are a mix of air and vacuum braked with two empty M.O.D. PFA Warflats, three VEA vans, a bogie bolster, four 45t bitumen tanks, a hopper wagon, VAA type van, BSW bogie bolster and a CAR brake van which is required as there is no through brake. 24th July 1985

Above - No 45058 is making a spirited departure from the yard at Severn Tunnel Junction with a north bound Speedlink working. The consist is eight loaded HEA coal hoppers, six VEA vans and a 100 ton bogie oil tanker. 7th May 1986.

Opposite top - One of the original named Western Region class 47s 47085 'Mammoth' heading west from Westbury with a short Speedlink working made up of a bogie Ferry Van, a covered steel wagon and some TTA bitumen tanks. In the left background can be seen Westbury Cement works and on the right the White Horse on the hill. 25th September 1987. John Dedman Collection.

Opposite bottom - No 33030 at Nursling with the Dinton/ Quidhampton to Eastleigh Speedlink feeder service consisting of five ECC china clay bogie tanks followed by four vans, a VDA, a VEA, another VDA and finally a VTG bogie ferry van. 33030 is filling in for a class 47 which is the usual class of loco for this turn. 13th February 1991. Photo by Peter Mantle.

No 47207 at Millbrook with the 6O42 08:30 Severn Tunnel Speedlink to Eastleigh on 13th June 1986. This service usually produced a good variety of wagons and this day was no exception. The MOD flats loaded with armoured cars are probably destined for Marchwood, HEA wagons loaded with coal, a BR VIX Ferry Van, a single bitumen tank for Fawley, a FMA set of three flat wagons and a selection of air braked vans including another ferry van. The FMA set is formed of three ex freightliner flats which were converted to carry lorry cabs. Photo by Peter Mantle.

On 11th April 1988 No 33021 is at Southampton with the 6Z00 13:25 Ashchurch to Eastleigh Speedlink, listed in the working timetable as a Q working, which runs as required. This is basically an M.O.D. train composed of a single VEA van followed by Warwell and Warflat wagons loaded with various military armoured vehicles. The likely eventual destination was Marchwood.

Right - An unidentified class 33/1 is passing Southampton Up Yard with the 6Y61 09:30 Marchwood to Salisbury Speedlink, the train is composed of four OAA wagons loaded with pipes and thirteen assorted air braked vans. 19th September 1986

Bottom - No 45040 is taking the 6V83 16:25 Speedlink to Severn Tunnel Junction from the East Yard to the station at Eastleigh where it will run round the stock before heading west towards Romsey. The wagons are in three groups, loaded bitumen tanks from Fawley, empty HEA coal hoppers and BDA bogie bolsters bringing up the rear. 29th March 1985.

No 33023 has left Fratton and is crossing Ports Creek as it approaches Portcreek Junction with one VDA van. The train is the 6Y51 09:38 Hove to Eastleigh Speedlink trip working which drops into Fratton for an hour and a half where wagons are exchanged and the loco has to run round. Photo by Pete Nurse.

No 33007 is heading along the Bedenham branch (the truncated remains of the former Fareham to Gosport line) with the 6T50 09:18 from Eastleigh. Behind the loco are nine VEA vans, the first of which is in early Railfreight maroon livery, the remaining in the later Railfreight red/grey livery. Photo by Pete Nurse.

No33001 is heading back to Eastleigh Yard with the 6Y51 09:38 Speedlink trip working from Hove, a light load with only two PWA UKF fertiliser vans. Photo by Pete Nurse.

Top - Nos 20060 and 20117 are heading south at Willington with two air braked vans, a VBA in red and grey livery and a VDA in yellow and grey livery. 2nd June 1988.

Bottom - Another pair of disc headcode class 20s Nos 20085 and 20040 have just left Toton Yard with a train of loaded HEA coal hoppers with two VCA vans included in the formation. The train is the 7A84 06:26 Toton Old Bank to Willesden Brent Sidings Speedlink, 16th July 1986.

Top - The four track main line north through the Erewash valley was a busy section for a variety of freight trains. On 4th July 1985, No 31188 is seen heading north near Heanor with a Speedlink working consisting of 45 ton oil tanks and various steel carrying wagons.

Bottom - At 05:45 on 16th July 1986 No 31117 has arrived at Toton with a Speedlink working, the train is made up of four sliding hood steel wagons and HEA and HAA empty coal hoppers amongst which is a bogie scrap wagon. Toton diesel depot is very busy at this time of day with locos of various classes leaving, the first of which is No 25190.

Above - Nos 37046 and 37106 are passing the signal box at Whitwell with the 6M70 17:30 Worksop to Toton Speedlink on the 3rd July 1985. The formation contains two loaded HEA coal wagons, two vans sandwiching an oil tank and about a dozen or so loaded HAA coal wagons.

Opposite top - Seen from a passing train No 08682 is shunting three Rockware Glass PCA wagons at Doncaster on 21st April 1987.

Opposite bottom - Winwick on the West Coast main line is a popular location for railway photographers and is the location as Nos 20034 and 20042 pass with nine empty HAA wagons and four Shell TTA tanks. 12th July 1990.

No 20127 is at Fort William Junction with five OBA wagons and a single BBA steel wagon on 10th August 1987. Being a Scottish allocated loco 20127 is fitted with miniature snowploughs. John Dedman Collection.

Coal Traffic

No 26039 is arriving at Mossend Yard with 21ton MDV mineral wagons on 8th August 1989. Photo by Peter Mantle.

Left - With four coal containers No 37244 is heading north from Mossend Yard at 07:50 on 10th July 1990.

Right - At 09:30 No 37244 is returning to the yard at Mossend with a single coal container. 10th July 1990.

On a very unseasonal wet morning No 37007 has charge of a short train of fourteen unfitted 16 ton coal wagons and a brake van at Bafferton near Darlington on 10th June 1980.

A pair of split headcode class 37s numbers Nos 37078 and 37242 are heading north on the East Coast Main Line at South Otterington with empty HAA wagons on 9th June 1980.

Well weathered large logo liveried No 56106 has charge of a southbound rake of empty HAA coal hoppers on the freight-only line at Whitwelll on 3rd July 1985. This line has been re-opened to passenger trains between Nottingham and Worksop and is known as the Robin Hood line. Unfortunately many of the freight only lines which mostly served coal mines in this area have since been closed.

No 20064 is seen at Hall Lane Junction with a morning trip from Barrow Hill to Bolsover Coalite. Behind the loco is a CAR air piped brake van followed by eight HEA and eleven HAA empty coal hoppers. 17th July 1986.

Nos 20048 in blue and 20010 in red stripe Railfreight livery have just passed Hall Lane Junction at Staveley. The train is a Barrow Hill to Bolsover Coalite trip working consisting of six empty HEA and HBA coal hoppers. 7th July 1987.

No 20214 is passing Hall Lane Junction for another trip down the Bolsover branch to collect more loaded coal hoppers which will be brought back to Barrow Hill yard for onward distribution. Behind the loco is a CAR air piped brake van in Speedlink red and grey livery for the guard to ride in, which was usual for single Class 20 operated trains on this branch. 4th July 1985.

On the 17th July 1986 No 20064 is passing Hall Lane Junction with a loaded train from Bolsover Coalite consisting of a CAR brake van and six HBA and HEA coal hoppers.

To p - 20064 is arriving at Barrow Hill yard with an air piped brake van and four loaded HAA coal hoppers from Bolsover Coalite. After arrival in the yard 20064 retired to the loco depot and the four HAAs were taken north by a pair of class 20 locos. 15th July 1986.

Bottom - Nos 20174 and 20107 are heading south at Clay Cross Junction on 4th July 1985 with loaded HEA and HBA coal hoppers. 20174 was later transferred to Thornaby Depot where it had the name 'Captain James Cook R.N.' painted on red solebars.

Top - Nos 20026 and 20070 are travelling through the Erewash Valley near Heanor with fifteen well loaded HBA and HEA coal hoppers. 4th July 1985.

Bottom - With Toton Diesel depot as the backdrop Nos 20144 and 20107 head north with three HEA and thirteen HAA empty coal hoppers. 20163 can just be seen waiting to propel its brake van out of the depot before heading south on the main line, fo'lowing that are two very clean class 58s waiting their turn to leave the depot. More locos of classes 20, 25, 45, 56 and 58 can be seen in the depot. 16th July 1986.

With a short rake of seven HAA coal hoppers Nos 20058 and 20188 have arrived at Toton on 7th July 1987. In the background locos of class 47 and 56 are waiting to depart from the depot. Locos of classes 20, 31, 37, 47, 56 and 58 can be seen in the depot. The refuelling point can be seen to the left side of the main depot building where there is a Railfreight liveried class 20.

A short coal train which would be of interest to railway modellers, is made up of six HEA and 2 HAA loaded coal hopper, loaded with various grades of coal. The locos are Nos 20197 and 20151 and are approaching Toton from the south on 15th July 1986.

Top - Nos 20004 and 20160 are heading south from Toton with two empty HBA coal hoppers bound for Rawden Colliery on the Coalville line. In the background is Toton wagon repair works where lines of HEA hoppers can be seen awaiting attention. 30th April 1987.

Bottom - As more powerful locos were introduced so Merry Go Round coal trains of HAA wagons got longer. By later standards No 47357 has a comparatively short rake of twenty four heading north near Willington on 11th June 1986.

No 45042 is heading south near Bedford with a loaded Merry Go Round train of HAA wagons, 14th September 1977.

As the sun is rising No 31183 is southbound on the East Coast main line at Sandy with four 16 ton mineral wagons loaded with coal with a brake van bringing up the rear. 14th September 1977.

Top - Narrow bodied class 33/2 No. 33208 is at Purley with a trainload of loaded HEA domestic coal wagons. 30th September 1988. John Dedman Collection.

Bottom - The sun is setting on the late evening Fratton to Didcot HEA coal empties as they cross Ports Creek on the approach to Portcreek Junction. The loco is No 37220. Photo by Pete Nurse.

Top - No 31246 is heading north at Churchdown with empty 16 ton mineral wagons and loaded 21 ton hoppers on 22nd July 1983.

Bottom - Having just crossed the Bishton flyover No 37159 is heading east towards Severn Tunnel Junction with twenty two loaded HBA and HEA coal hoppers in a mixture of Bauxite and Railfreight red liveries. 24th July 1985.

Steel and Metals

Top - With six BDA bogie bolster wagons in tow, No 37239 has just come off the Bishton Flyover and is heading towards Severn Tunnel Junction on 24th July 1985. No 37239 was later repainted in Railfreight Coal Sector livery and named 'The Coal Merchants Association of Scotland'.

Bottom - Newport is in the background as Nos 56001 and 56052 are heading west to Port Talbot from Llanwern steelworks with a train of empty iron ore tippler wagons. 6th May 1986.

A pair of class 20s led by No 20096 are heading south at Portway north of Tamworth with a single BBA wagon loaded with steel coil on 15th September 1987.

Nos 20002+20098 heading north with an SPA and a BBA at Willington on 7th September 1987. The empty HAA wagons are part of an MGR service waiting to leave the Power Station.

One of Thornaby Depot's class 37s no. No 37095 is heading south at Stenson Junction with ten BBA wagons loaded with steel slabs. The Thornaby depot markings are the white cantrail stripe and the bodyside white kingfisher logo. 7th September 1987.

No 37030 is approaching Clay Cross Junction with a light weight 6M97 08:22 Tinsley to Wolverhampton Steel Terminal train. The wagons are an SPA and a BAA -making a good candidate for a model. 4th July 1985.

This page and opposite top - Nos 20117 and 20169 have just crossed the River Trent on the combined road and rail King George V lifting bridge at Althorpe. The bridge was built in 1916 and was last lifted in 1956. The two locos have a light load of one BVW steel coil wagon carrying two coils which can be seen in the second view. 9th June 1992

Opposite bottom - Nos 20035 and 20076 at Helsby with empty BBA steel wagons from the British Steel works at Shotton. 2nd May 1986. John Dedman Collection.

Top - Two of Thornaby Depot's colourful class 20s numbers Nos 20172 and 20028 are passing South Bank on Teeside with Limestone empties from Redcar which are heading for Redmire for reloading. 20172 has the name 'Redmire' painted on the red sole bar and large bodyside numbers, 20028 carries the name 'Bedale' on a black nameplate on the front end of the solebar. 5th July 1988.

Bottom - No 37098 is heading for Lackenby steelworks at South Bank with two Sliding Hood steel coil wagons and BDA bogie bolsters, most of which are loaded with steel slabs. 5th July 1988.

Petroleum

Top - Two locos and two wagons, Nos 20042 and 20034 are heading south at Winwick on the West Coast Main Line with two Shell TTA tanks on 12th July 1990. The two tanks have lost their conventional drab grey livery and have been repainted into the new Shell livery with the red and yellow stripes.

Bottom - No 47318 has charge of a train of BP 100ton tanks forming the 6V69 10:20 Gainsborough to Llandarcy south of Abbotswood Junction near Worcester 22nd July 1983

No 45009 is heading west from Newport with ten TTA tanks on 7th May 1986.

No 47125 is approaching Newport from the west with five Acetic acid tanks . 7th May 1986.

On Mayday 1981 No 47246 heads east near Cholsey on the Great Western Main Line with a train of eleven Gulf tank cars with a barrier wagon behind the loco. It is the 6A18 04:45 Robeston sidings to Theale. Photo by Dave Payne.

No 33105 has just left Eastleigh East Yard with the 6B80 13:33 departure to Esso Fawley, the empty wagons are TTAs for diesel oil and TSA bitumen tanks. The East Yard can be seen in the background with 47338 waiting to leave with a ballast train. On the right hand side is a fenced private siding where ICI methanol tanks are unloaded with reach wagons parked outside of the gate. 29th March 1985.

Large logo liveried class 47/4 No. 47450 is leaving the tunnel under Southampton City Centre with the 6B72 13:10 Fawley to Eastleigh tanks. The third wagon is a liquid chlorine tank sandwiched between the usual Esso TTAs. 16th June 1988.

No 47351 is accelerating through St Denys station after a signal check with a dozen empty 100ton bogie LPG tanks forming the 6O32 05:56 Longport to Southampton Down yard. The tanks will be tripped to the Fawley Refinery on a later service. 16th June 1988.

Top - No 47146 has charge of a lengthy train of tanks from Fawley as it approaches Southampton on 11th April 1988. The first ten wagons are class A TTAs followed by a barrier wagon and a liquid chlorine tank. These are followed by more TTAs a with a few bitumen tanks bringing up the rear.

Bottom - No 47369 is passing through Hythe on the Fawley branch with the 6W62 12:02 from Furzebrook Oil Sidings which served the Wytch Farm oil field in Dorset. The wagons are BP TEA bogie tanks carrying crude oil for refining at the Esso Fawley Refinery. These trains were running twice a day until 1989 when a pipeline was installed from Furzebrook to BP's depot at Hamble, the crude oil was then transported by ship to BPs refinery in South Wales. 21st March 1988.

Cement

Nos 33102 and 33107 are heading across Bishop's Dyke towards Beaulieu Road station with twenty CPV pressflo's forming the twice weekly 6V94 18.32 Poole to Westbury Blue Circle cement . Unfortunately in 2013 this vantage point is now overgrown and covered in trees and scrub. 19th July 1979.

A once a week train through Eastleigh is the 6Y40 10:10 Southampton Down Yard to Northfleet B.C.I. Normally a Wednesday only service, on this occasion it was running on Friday 13th June 1986. No 33031 is hauling eleven Blue Circle PDA bogie cement wagons which by this date have had their company logos removed. Photo by Peter Mantle.

No 47409 'David Lloyd George' is approaching Millbrook, Southampton with a light load of three very clean PCA cement wagons. This was a Gateshead loco and was withdrawn later that year, the name plates were only carried for one year. 19th June 1986. Photo by Keith Mantle.

No 73108 is passing Worting Junction with the 6Y80 09:46 Southampton Up Yard to Halling on Saturday 30th June 1984. The wagons are Rugby Cement PCA cement wagons.

Left - No 47328 is near Portway north of Tamworth with the 6M18 16:05 Earles Sidings to Greaves Sidings Cement. The wagons are mostly PCA with three PDA bogie wagons mixed into the formation. 19th June 1986

This page bottom and opposite top - Class 20s 20133 and 20160 are heading south from Toton Yard with two PCA cement wagons on 15th July 1986.

Opposite bottom - On 10th July 1990 No 26027 is pulling out of the up yard at Mossend with fourteen PCA cement wagons. As usual there are a good selection of wagons in the sidings of the yard.

No 47349 is pulling out of the sidings at Peak Forest with a good selection of four wheeled cement wagons and a bogie hopper, 16th July 1986.

No 47145 is heading south from Peak Forest towards Tunstead with two Clyde Cement PBA Covhop wagons. 8th July 1987.

Stone

Top - No 37106 is reversing two bogie stone hoppers and a brake van on to the short branch leading to the quarry at Whitwell where a type of stone called Dolamite was excavated. 4th July 1985

Bottom - No 37106 is now leaving the branch with the brake van after depositing the two hoppers at the quarry.

Left - No 47314 is at St Denys with the Westbury to Totton loaded PGA stone hoppers, 25th September 1986.

Opposite top - On 23rd June 1982 No 46023 is approaching Westbury from the north with a train of loaded MSV stone wagons. Photo by Dave Payne.

Opposite bottom - First of its class **No** 56001 is heading along the single track near Crampmoor with the 6V81 16:00 Eastleigh to Merehead Quarry with empty Yeoman PGA stone hoppers on 13th September 1985.

Taking the route to Westbury at Fairwood Junction is No 56034 with a loaded stone train. It has come from Merehead Quarry and the wagons are Yeoman and Tarmac PGA hoppers. No 56034 was later named 'Castell Ogwr / Ogmore Castle'. 6th June 1984

No 47112 is coming off the Romsey line at Eastleigh with loaded ARC stone tipplers on 29th March 1985. On the right the 6E30 17:19 Eastleigh to Tyne Yard Speedlink is about to depart, with a VEA Van, a VDA van, an ICI Methanol TTA and seven VDA vans, the last six with white roofs. These vans were normally used for Rowntrees traffic and the white roofs were to help keep the van contents cool.

Departmental

No 33057 fitted with miniature snowploughs is at Beaulieu Road with ballast for works near Lymington Junction. The train has come from Eastleigh and will berth at Brockenhurst until required. Looks like all the wagons are the welded later type Seacows which are available ready to run in 00 gauge. 9th April 1988. Photo by Peter Mantle

No 33111 has charge of thirteen loaded Seacow bogie ballast wagons at East Grimstead on 18th May 1984. It is the 7Y56 10:33 Salisbury to Three Bridges, the wagons were loaded at Meldon Quarry in Devon from where they departed the previous day.

Top - A view of Eastleigh from the top of the multi-storey car park sees No 33032 arriving with empty wagons on 19th April 1985. A selection of wagons are on view in the yard along with some withdrawn electric multiple units. The railway works seen in the background is still busy in 2013 with repairs and overhauls for various privatised railway companies.

Bottom - No 50046 'Ajax' on Departmental duties at Westbury on the 5th April 1990. Behind the loco is a Dutch liveried Shark ballast plough van followed by a dozen Dogfish ballast wagons, only two of which are in the more modern Dutch grey and yellow livery.

Top - With an audience on the platform, No 37306 is growling through Castle Cary station with a loaded ballast train at 9:10am on 28th July 1984. The six Seacow wagons are a mix of departmental liveries with four in Dutch grey/yellow and two in well weathered olive green. Photo by Dave Payne.

Right - No 45049 is heading north past Barrow Hill with the 8E69 10:05 Loughborough ARC to York loaded ballast train. Wagons include Dogfish, Catfish and Sealion. 17th July 1986.

Opposite top - No 37031 is heading south at Foxlow Junction on 4th July 1985 with a mixed set of empty Dogfish and Catfish ballast wagons.

Opposite bottom - No 31142 is passing Doveholes quarry at Peak Forest with five loaded Sealion ballast wagons on 16th July 1986.

No 26011 is seen near Polmont Junction with seven empty Turbot wagons. 7th August 1989. Photo by Peter Mantle.

Acknowledgements and References:

Ian Allan Motive Power ABC's, Platform 5 Locomotives & Coaching Stock, John Fox collection of timetables.
Peter Mantle, Keith Mantle, Pete Moody, Dave Payne, Pete Nurse, British Railways Mark 1 Coaches by Keith Parkin.

Wagon photos and information at:-
http://paulbartlett.zenfolio.com/paulbartlettsrailwaywagons

Class 47 locos http://www.brushtype4.co.uk/bt4_intro.php
Class 50 locos http://www.class50.com/c50_intro.php

Class 50 locos http://www.fiftyfund.org.uk/index.htm